Ethical Leadership

Leadership for a New Millennium

by
Michael C. Pickett

authorHOUSE™

1663 LIBERTY DRIVE, SUITE 200
BLOOMINGTON, INDIANA 47403
(800) 839-8640
WWW.AUTHORHOUSE.COM

First published by AuthorHouse 07/26/05

ISBN: 1-4208-4713-9 (sc)

Library of Congress Control Number: 2005903448

Printed in the United States of America
Bloomington, Indiana

This book is printed on acid-free paper.

Table of Contents

Dedication

To my wife Evette and daughter Jenna for their unlimited support and understanding whose patient love enabled me to complete this book.

Acknowledgements

Knowing trees, I understand the meaning of patience.
Knowing grass, I can appreciate persistence.
Hal Boreland (1842 –1914)

As with any journey, there are many that make lasting impressions on our lives and I would like to acknowledge the following professors that I had the pleasure of learning from their collective wisdom.

Firstly, Dr. Michele Stimac, Pepperdine University, from whom I have learned a great deal more than I can ever hope to put into words and Dr. Terrence Deal, University of Southern California, whose organizational insights are boundless.

I would also like to acknowledge Dr. Will McWhinney, co-founder of The Fielding Institute, whose creativity is as limitless as his energy given so freely to doctoral students.

Last, but not least, I would like to thank the legendary Dr. Paul Hersey, founder of The Center for Leadership Studies, for taking the time from an extremely busy schedule to review my early ideas.

Prologue

Ethics — the values by which human beings live in relation to other human beings, nature, God, and themselves.
— Jacques P. Thiroux

The mere mention of ethics in today's organizations can generate sensitivity in even the most judicious leaders as a result of many highly publicized recent organizational debacles. It is not the intent of this book to recant the recent organizational fiascos that seem to grow exponentially as the global economy places increased financial burdens on the profitability of the varying industries.

The model for ethical leadership that is presented in this book is the result of many years of research in organizational ethics in addition to paradoxical daily observations of behaviors that are typically incongruent to published organizational codes of ethics and in many cases incongruent with deeply held values. It is my hope that the leadership model presented in this book will provide the impetus for leaders and managers in all types of organizations to take a moment to reflect upon how their individuality relates to the espoused organizational values as they pursue their daily tasks and responsibilities.

MCP

Introduction

Watch your thoughts; they become words. Watch your words; they become actions. Watch your actions; they become habits. Watch your habits; they become character. Watch your character; it becomes your destiny.
— Unknown

Organizations today are finding themselves continually struggling with ethical and moral dilemmas as evidenced in the news media. Many organizations have ethics programs in place to satisfy the "gray" areas between economic necessity, legal obligations, environmental responsibilities, and social responsibilities. Also, organizations that have established ethics codes commonly are taken by surprise when ethical dilemmas arise and employees' behaviors do not meet the desired expectations. How can this paradox possibly occur?

Metaphorically, this scenario is likened to the tale of the three blind men and the elephant, each with their own perspective, none of which is seeing the whole picture, much like espoused theories versus theories-in-use (Senge, 1994). Espoused theories are what individuals assert when describing or trying to justify behaviors, whereas theory-in-use is the actual behavior as determined by observations. Ethics programs often give "situational" codes of conduct to employees; yet when employees are faced with similar dilemmas, observed behavior is somewhat contrary.

Kohlberg's (1983) ethical dilemma scenarios, which determine an individual's cognitive moral development (CMD), help to explain one's espoused theory versus theory-in-use. In other words, Kohlberg's theory helps to clarify the "why" behind observed behavior. Thus, understanding the "why" behind one's espoused theory explains more closely what we observe during an individual's theory-in-use. This context of this book is based upon this basic understanding of human behavior.

Evolution of Management and Leadership

By standing on the shoulders of great men, you are able to see farther.
– Paul Hersey

Extensive research has been conducted in leadership (Bass, 1990; Hersey & Blanchard, 1988; Senge 1990; Senge, et al, 1994; Wheatley, 1994), business ethics and social responsibility (Carroll, 1996), to mention only a few. While conducting a search of the relevant literature in general, I discovered that it revealed a philosophical and scholarly character. Upon reflection, I realized three distinct polarizations. It is not my intention to marginalize scholarly work but only to seek to provide a philosophical basis from which to begin a discourse in the analysis required to operationalize a model for ethical leadership.

To provide a structural foundation with which to begin this book, the aforementioned research can be categorized into descriptive, proscriptive and, prescriptive ideologies. The purpose for providing this structural foundation is to develop an understanding of how current research has evolved and to argue for the need to expand scholarly thinking regarding the application of theories in organizations. This expanded thinking will incorporate the notion of praxis in the practical application of theory. Praxis comes from the Greek word "prassein", to pass through; taken more practically to mean an exercise or practice of an art, science or skill. In essence, the praxis of ethical leadership will include a skillful synthesis and application of many leadership, management and ethical theories. In this regard the leader becomes a scholar-practitioner. A requisite of a scholar-practitioner is an epistemological integration of theory and practice. In other words, the researcher argues that one cannot effectively apply theory void of understanding.

The examples that follow are not intended to be all-inclusive, but only a flavoring of the trend of relevant research.

Descriptive Ideology

The descriptive ideology includes aspects pertaining to the qualitative nature of a discipline. In other words, characterizations that may either be illustrative, expressive or interpretive.

An illustrative characterization is a description that serves as a representation of a general theory. Examples of this ideology are the trait and great-man leadership theories.

Bass (1990) in his seminal text, *Bass and Stogdill's Handbook of Leadership*, found early leadership studies focused on a descriptive approach. Included within the research were the great-man and trait theories. These early leadership theories differentiated superior qualities, traits, and differing degrees of intelligence, moral force and heredity. In contrast, I found the notion of descriptive ideology in the field of ethics extremely limited. This is a reasonable finding since ethics is grounded in relational terms, i.e., ethics is essentially reflective conduct. However, a descriptive, ethics-related discussion can be traced to Plato's dialog in Meno (Jowett, 1995).

Expressive or interpretive descriptive ideologies articulate clear distinctions among theories. An example of this ideology is found in the research presented by Rokeach (1973) in values.

Highly related to ethics is Rokeach's (1973) seminal work *The Nature of Human Values* in which Rokeach (1973, pp. 325-26) states that the theoretical implications of the descriptive studies in human values that have been accomplished provide the:

1) conceptual distinctiveness of terminal and instrumental values
2) conceptual place of values in the behavioral sciences

3) role that social institutions play in instilling and maintaining human values, and

4) validity of conflicting theories of personality development and of Maslow's hierarchical theory of motivation.

Additionally, important contemporary social psychological theoretical implications are mentioned in regard to "...attitudes, short-term change, persuasion, and consistency between cognitive elements" (Rokeach, 1973, p. 326). These implications raise questions for future research in the behavioral sciences, social institutions, personality development and theories of change.

Proscriptive Ideology

The proscriptive ideology is not intended to imply necessarily negative theoretical connotations in the areas of leadership and ethics. The proscriptive ideology is exclusive or restrictive in nature; in other words, by choosing one leadership style or theoretical foundation to follow, one does not choose the remaining choices. A visual representation of this ideology, taken from elementary probability theory, is that of a Venn diagram in which there is a single circle labeled "A". The area within the circle is "A" the area outside of the circle is "not A". McGregor (Bass, 1990) provides a practical example to demonstrate this phenomenon. By identifying oneself as a Theory Y manager, one is excluded, through an individual, cognitive choice, not to identify oneself as a Theory X manager.

Various management schools of thought are identified within this ideology such as the philosophy of Taylor's scientific management (Wrege & Greenwood, 1991) in addition to Fayol's qualities of a manager (Wren, 1994, p. 183):

1. Physical qualities: health, vigor, address.
2. Mental qualities: ability to understand and learn, judgment, mental vigor, and adaptability.
3. Moral qualities: energy, firmness, willingness to accept responsibility, initiative, loyalty, tact, dignity.
4. General education: general acquaintance with matters not belonging exclusively to the functions performed.
5. Special knowledge: that peculiar to the function, be it technical, commercial, financial, managerial and so on.
6. Experience: knowledge arising from the work proper, the recollection of lessons a person has derived from things.

The proscriptive ideology provides a critical link in our growth in understanding and theory development. This link enables a cognitive, evolutionary phase in which research is transformed from a descriptive view, which is based on qualitative properties, to the situatedness of the prescriptive ideology, or that which is a reality-based application of theoretical constructs (See Figure 1).

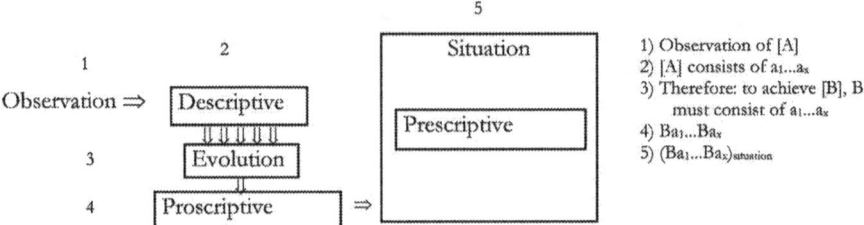

Figure 1. The theoretical construct and relationships of the tripartite ideologies

---

Note: The theoretical construct and relationships of the tripartite ideologies include descriptive, proscriptive and prescriptive theory. Descriptive theory is based upon observation. Proscriptive theory results from an evolution consisting of cognitive deconstruction, reconstruction and universal application of the qualitative descriptive theory. Prescription results from the acknowledgment and perspective that theoretical application is situation specific.

Proscription, as represented in Figure 1, demonstrates the subtleties of human nature that leads us to deconstruct what we can describe, define, or recognize qualitatively in order to reconstruct these qualities in such a way that provides a transformation into a notion that is applied universally. To explain this phenomenon further, let us assume that good leaders are found to have the qualities of dependability, initiative and adaptability. From a proscriptive ideology, to be a good leader one must be dependable, adaptable and initiating.

Some examples that demonstrate the proscriptive ideology are McGregor's Theory X and Theory Y, Blake and Moutons' Managerial Grid, Bernard's executive functions (Wren, 1994), and the philosophy of deontological ethics. McGregor (Bass, 1990; Wren, 1994) developed two types of leadership thought, Theory X, and Theory Y. A Theory X leadership style is based on the assumption that the leader needs to direct passive, resistant subordinates to meet organizational goals; whereas, a Theory Y leadership style yields the belief that the subordinates are inherently motivated, enthusiastic and willing to accept responsibility (Bass, 1990).

Similarly, Blake and Mouton (Bass, 1990) theorized a managerial grid in which one axis represents concern for people and the other concern for production. The managerial grid is representative of the leadership school of thought that there is one effective style of leadership.

Lastly, from within the leadership and management examples, Chester Barnard's (Wren, 1994) functions of the executive provide a framework in which proscribe the successful performance of duties.

An ethics-related proscriptive example is argued from a deontological perspective. Kant's categorical imperative reasons that one should act as if the maxim from which you act were to be as though you will a universal law (Kant, 1790).

Viewing universal application of theory through critical, reflective analysis we see the inherent disconnect between perceived reality and proscription. An example of this concept is illustrated by a Theory X manager, or one that views employees as needing to be directed. Managing employees that are self-directed and autonomous from within a Theory X managerial perception may not be effective. Hence, the prescriptive ideology provides a natural cognitive migration that enables useful and practical application of theoretical concepts that are situation specific (See Figure 1).

Prescriptive Ideology

The prescriptive ideology adds situational factors to the application of theory (See Figure 1). In contrast to proscriptive theory, which applies one universal theory to all, prescriptive theory is individualized and context specific. The examples that follow demonstrate that situational components are not necessarily environmentally oriented and that situational context may even apply to individual psychological components.

Hersey and Blanchard's (1988; Bass, 1990) situational leadership argues that a leader's behavior is dependent on the follower's willingness and maturity level. Similar to Hersey and Blanchard's focus the individual, Fiedler's (Bass, 1990) contingency theory identifies a leader's effectiveness from within a context of task-oriented versus relations-oriented depending on the particular circumstances of a situation to include task structure, group relations and level of leader power. Whereas, House's path-goal theory uses goal clarification in combination with competence levels of followers and environmental forces (Bass, 1990). Lastly, group considerations were proposed by Yukl's (1989) multiple linkage model. Yukl's (1989) model considered subordinate's effort, skill, leader's role, resources available and the group's cohesiveness in any particular situation to determine leader behavior.

From the psychological perspective, Maslow (Bass, 1990) posited a theory of eupsychian management. Eupsychian management identified the need for management to develop "...subordinate's self-esteem and psychological health and emphasized the need for self-actualization so that everyone would have the opportunity to become what he or she had the capacity to become" (p. 44). According to this theory:

> ...the unconscious and the depths of personality
> have to be probed in the search for enlightened
> management. On the basis of these probes, different
> leaders will be chosen for different situations.

Many ethical theoretical positions exist in this ideology. However, to name a few, utilitarianism determines the rightness or wrongness of an action based on the goodness or badness of the perceived consequences. In contrast, the ethical egoist seek that which is in their own self-interest, while the relativist's view considers moralities relevant to individual societies.

What does this mean?

Understanding the behavioral nature of our propensity to categorize and compartmentalize ideas helps us focus on the overall philosophical underpinnings surrounding the nature of leadership and management theory. Describing and mentioning a small sampling of the last centuries' major works is not acted upon in haste with intent to marginalize great thinkers' work. In contrast, the focus of this chapter is to highlight the achievements of the last century and develop a greater understanding of the evolution of the various schools of thought and how they might apply to the development of an additional school of thought, that of ethical leadership. I believe, based on years of organizational observations, the managerial and leadership capabilities that exist in today's organizations are in need of a restructuring, not just another face lift.

By "face lift" I refer to the "flavor-of-the-month" new management crazes that typically sweep through organizations; identified by heightened awareness by the HR and training departments; that result in employee cynicism, management's half-hearted attempts and overall decreasing satisfaction with the work environment.

By restructuring management and leadership thought, the very philosophical essence of the application of theory changes its meaning. In other words, management and leadership behavior is based on outcomes assessment; meaning that organizational behaviors are adapted to the desired outcomes, based on individual organizational norms and mores. It is in this capacity that each individual organization will "fit" their management and leadership needs to their desired outcomes.

Why a Tripartite Ideology?

This journey to find a model for the praxis of ethical leadership may be likened to the start of many journeys. A path, while clear and intuitive to one, may not appear as a clear path to another as all of our individual passions lead us down different paths. However, while the goal in this journey is openly stated, this short introductory section provides a background that this researcher uses to establish a need for the development of a model for the praxis of ethical leadership in organizations.

Chapter 2

Understanding Ethics and Morality

The ancestor of every action is a thought.
— *Ralph Waldo Emerson*

A large portion of the ethics-related literature is highly philosophical. Throughout this review of literature, an effort will be made to be as succinct and as direct as possible in developing the relevance and application of various theoretical underpinnings. For this reason, a liberal use of tables will help to provide additional clarity of the ethical notions.

An Historical Foundation

Aristotle (McKeon, 1970), in *Nicomachean Ethics*, claims that morality cannot be learned by simply reading a treatise on virtue. The implication of Aristotle's observation is a cornerstone in the foundation of morality. Building upon this thesis, Aristotle asserts that the spirit of morality is awakened in the individual only through witnessing conduct of a moral person.

Teleology Versus Deontology

There are numerous theoretical schools of thought in ethics; however, each theory can be categorized as either teleological or deontological. According to Boyce & Jenson (1978), teleology "...implies direction toward a goal or some specific end state" (p. 21). In other words, theories from this perspective argue that an act is "...morally right or obligatory insofar as it tends to produce some desired end" (p. 21). That is to say, "...the rightness of an act depends solely on its consequences" (p. 21).

In contrast, deontology indicates that the nature of the act determines the morality of the act,

> [The]...nature of the act may mean a number of things. For instance, suppose one believes that moral principles are eternal and immutable and that these principles at least partially define moral action. Then, to determine the rightness of a given act one must determine its degree of conformity to moral principle(s). (p. 45)

In other words, justifying one's act based on an "end justifies the means" is not appropriate from the deontological school of thought; as the rightness or wrongness of an action depends on its individual correspondence to one's duty. Plainly, each means is an end unto itself.

Ethics and Moral Reasoning

Ethics and moral reasoning can be fraught with complex and enmeshed theoretical avenues. To develop a basic understanding, Boyce and Jenson (1978) posit that,

> . . .if one wishes to insure the acceptability of specific moral judgments and choices, then he [or she] must be quite aware of all moral assumptions that underlie them, and, insofar as possible, be assured of their correctness as well. (p. 6)

According to Boyce and Jenson, moral reasoning is composed of content and structure. A clear distinction is developed between these two terms in that "...content refers to what an individual believes while structure refers to the cognitive basis of those attitudes and beliefs" (p. 6).

Normative Ethics, Metaethics and Descriptive Ethics

Ethics, as viewed by Boyce and Jenson (1978), is divided into three major categories or philosophies, normative ethics, metaethics, and descriptive ethics. The different concepts of normative ethics, metaethics, and descriptive ethics, while distinct in their own way, become somewhat complex and convoluted due to seemingly minor differences. However, these differences become extremely important in ethical interpretation and application.

Normative Ethics. Table 1 describes Boyce and Jenson's (1978) first category, normative ethics.

According to Boyce and Jenson (1978), normative ethics "...refers to those moral assumptions or statements that are evaluative; they are one's basic underlying assumptions about what is right and wrong" (p. 7).

Table 1

Normative Ethics: Three-Tier Formation of Logic and Applied Logical Extension

Logic Formation	Logical Extension
a) Evaluative statement	We really ought to do away with Mom. (She's in so much pain.)
b) Maxim	People who are in great pain ought to be done away with. Life is not worth living when one is always in pain.
c) Normative statement	Pain is bad and ought to be avoided; pleasure is good ought to be sought.

Note. Adapted from Boyce, W.D. & Jenson, L.C. (1978). *Moral reasoning: a psychological-philosophical integration.* Lincoln, NB: University of Nebraska Press.

Usually, these judgments are implicit, and can be explicitly exposed only by logical extension" (p. 7). In other words, logic formation, or, more specifically, how one forms logical reasoning based on one's underlying assumptions, and the logical extensions, or the applied notion of one's assumptions, referred to in Table 1 begin with an evaluative statement. The evaluative statement is then developed into a generalized maxim, which is then formulated into a normative statement, which "...is the moral assumption upon which the person's more specific judgments are based..." (Boyce & Jenson, 1978, p. 8).

Metaethics. The category of metaethics, on the other hand, "...is concerned with the justification of one's basic moral assumptions or normative stance (Boyce & Jenson, p. 8). Metaethics is more analytical and epistemological. Stated differently, metaethics tries to identify how one justifies what one thinks is right.

Descriptive Ethics. Boyce and Jenson's (1978) final category, descriptive ethics, "...refers to specific judgments, decisions and actions of individuals in relation to particular events" (p. 9). An example of descriptive ethics is illustrated in Table 1, statement (a) "We really ought to do away with Mom (She's in so much pain)." According to Boyce and Jenson (1978), the concept of descriptive ethics is assumed to be congruent in normative ethics. For example, in the above statement, "She's in so much pain" describes an underlying normative base.

Normative Ethics and Concepts of Value

To avoid confusion, Boyce and Jenson (1978) divided values into the categories of instrumental and intrinsic.

Instrumental Values. Boyce and Jenson's (1978) concept of instrumental value includes those "...who reject the existence of intrinsic goodness usually argue that there is no real distinction between end and means" (p. 14). In other words, instrumental values do not necessarily pertain to specific end states.

In contrast, Rokeach (1973), with a more functional definition, differentiates the concept of "values" with the terms instrumental and terminal. Terminal values are seen as the final goal or end state. Instrumental values are seen as the means to an end state; whereas, from a more theoretical perspective, Boyce and Jenson (1978) posit that instrumental values are defined in terms of goodness.

Dewey (cited in Boyce & Jenson, 1978, pp. 14-15) argued that:

> Means are means; they are intermediates, middle terms. To grasp this fact is to have done with the ordinary dualism of means and ends. The "end" is merely a series of acts viewed at a remote stage; and a means is merely the series viewed at an earlier one. Means and ends are two names for the same reality but a distinction in judgment. The first or earliest means is the most important to discover...

More clearly stated, if one's final reality is that of war, the intermediate stages, or individual battles, describe Dewey's distinction.

Rokeach (1973) states that when we speak of values, or, "When we say that a person has a value, we have in mind either his [her] beliefs concerning desirable modes of conduct or desirable end states of existence" (p. 7). Rokeach (1973) also defines two categories of instrumental values, moral and competence. Moral values refer to modes of behavior which necessarily do not relate to end states of behavior (Rokeach, 1973). Whereas, "Competence, or self-actualizing values have a personal focus" (p. 8).

Intrinsic Values. Aristotle, in opposition with Dewey's philosophy that there is "no intrinsically good thing (Boyce & Jenson, 1978), believed that intrinsic value consists of end states that can be good in and of themselves:

> The final good is thought to be self-sufficient...the self sufficient we now define as that which when isolated makes life desirable and lacking in nothing; and such happiness to be; and further we think it most desirable of all things, without being counted as one good among others...happiness, then, is something final and self-sufficient, and is the end of action. (p. 15)

In the above excerpt, Aristotle represents a monist's point of view as opposed to a pluralist's perspective. Monists argue "...that only one thing is intrinsically good...", whereas a "...pluralist asserts that two or more things are intrinsically good" (Boyce & Jenson, 1978, p. 16).

Normative Value Versus Moral Obligation

Moral value-based judgments are concerned with "goodness" or "badness" (Table 2). As displayed in Table 2, Boyce and Jenson (1978) posit that there are two categories of goodness or badness, that of being either particular or general. The more particular instances pertain to personalized, specific instances as opposed to the more generalized value-based judgment statements.

Table 2
Normative Ethics: Judgments of Value
Judgments of Moral Value (good and bad)

Particular	General
a) My Grandfather was a good man.	a) Benevolence is a virtue.
b) Xavier was a saint.	b) Jealousy is an ignoble motive.
c) Her character is admirable.	c) The ideally good man does not drink or smoke.

Note. Adapted from Boyce, W.D. & Jenson, L.C. (1978). *Moral reasoning: a psychological-philosophical integration.* Lincoln, NB: University of Nebraska Press.

Moral obligation-based judgments are concerned with the "rightness" or "wrongness" of a judgment (Table 3). The subtleties between moral value and moral obligation is the "should do" versus the "ought to do," respectively. A moral value, typically identifiable by "should," juxtaposes a value-laden connotation upon the statement which is very different than implying what "ought" to be done based on societal inference of the prevailing norms.

Table 3

Normative Ethics: Judgments of Obligation (Judgments of Moral Obligation (right and wrong))

Particular	General
a) I ought to escape from prison now.	a) We ought to keep our appointments.
b) You should become a missionary.	b) Love is the fulfillment of moral law.
c) What he did was wrong.	c) All men have a right to freedom.

Note. Adapted from Boyce, W.D. & Jenson, L.C. (1978). *Moral reasoning: a psychological-philosophical integration.* Lincoln, NB: University of Nebraska Press.

The Components of Morality

Rest (1984) points out that previous theoretical approach to morality focused on three constructs, behavior, affect and cognition. He argues that this three-fold distinction is deficient, and proposes a four-component model to identify the inner processes producing behavior.

Table 4 presents the major functions of the four components of morality comprising the inner processes of moral behavior as Rest identifies them.

While the four components of the inner processes of moral behavior appear to be linear, Rest (1984) maintains that moral behavior is not a "unitary process," and moral behavior reflects and derives from the "four inner cognitive-affective processes" (p.29). In addition, Rest describes external influences on the four inner components. These situational factors drawn from previous research are displayed for each component in Tables 5 through 8.

Table 4
Inner Processes of Moral Behavior

Component	Major Functions
1	a) Interpret the situation in terms of how one's actions affect the welfare of others.
2	a) Formulate what a moral course of action would be.
	b) Identify the moral ideal in a specific situation.
3	a) Select among competing value outcomes of ideals, the one to act on.
	b) Deciding whether or not to try to fulfill one's moral ideal.
4	a) Execute and implement what one intends to do.

Note. Adapted from Rest, J.R. *The major components of morality* in Kurtines, W.M. & Gewirtz, J.L. (1984). *Morality, moral behavior, and moral development.* New York: John Wiley & Sons.

For each of the four inner processes of moral behavior, Rest (1984) argues that moral behavior involves the use of all four components and that "...deficiencies in any component can result in failure to behave morally" (p. 36).

Situational Influences of Component 1

Table 5 depicts various situational factors that influence Component 1, the interpretation of a situation in terms of how one's actions affect the welfare of others. How a person views the effect of his/her behavior on others is influenced by the subjective perception of the ambiguity of various people's needs, the time allotted for interpreting the specific situation to the degree of personal danger, and one's susceptibility to pressure in a given situation, to just name a few. However, when taken in the context of an organizational setting, these factors provide a truly individualized environment for each employee. In other words, while the environmental cues of workload, goals and deadlines are expressed somewhat equally for all employees, each individual employee's cognitive interpretation of "their" situation makes the perception unique.

Table 5
Situational Factors That Influence Component One

Component 1

Interpret the situation in terms of how one's actions affect the welfare of others.

Influences
a) Ambiguity of people's needs, intentions and actions.
b) Familiarity with the situation or the people in it.
c) Time allowed for interpretation.
d) Degree of personal danger and susceptibility to pressure.
e) Preoccupation with other component processes.
f) Sheer number of elements in the situation and the embeddedness of crucial cues.
g) Complexity in tracing out cause-effect chains.
h) Presuppositions and prior expectations that blind a person to notice or think about certain aspects.

Note. Adapted from Rest, J.R. *The major components of morality* in Kurtines, W.M. & Gewirtz, J.L. (1984). *Morality, moral behavior, and moral development.* New York: John Wiley & Sons.

Situational Influences of Component 2

The second component of the inner processes of moral behavior has two aspects: a) formulate what a moral course of action would be and, b) identify the moral ideal in a specific situation. Table 6 summarizes the environmental influences associated with this inner process. They include the delegating of responsibilities, factors affecting the application of particular social norms or moral ideals, or their "activation," and prior conditions, promises, contracts, or expectancies that affect role responsibilities, reciprocity, or deservingness. Lastly, the preempting of one's sense of fairness by prior commitments to some ideology or code infers a large role in various organizational cultures that currently espouse local codes of ethics.

Table 6
Situational Factors That Influence Component Two

Component 2

a) Formulate what a moral course of action would be.

b) Identify the moral ideal in a specific situation.

　Influences

　　a)　Factors affecting the application of particular social norms or moral ideals, or their "activation".

　　b)　Delegation of responsibility to someone else.

　　c)　Prior conditions, promises, contracts, or expectancies that affect role responsibilities, reciprocity, or deservingness.

　　d)　The particular combination of moral issues involved.

　　e)　Preempting of one's sense of fairness by prior commitments to some ideology or code.

Note. Adapted from Rest, J.R. *The major components of morality* in Kurtines, W.M. & Gewirtz, J.L. (1984). *Morality, moral behavior, and moral development.* New York: John Wiley & Sons.

Situational Influences of Component 3

The third aspect of the inner processing of moral behavior consists of selecting among competing outcomes of ideals, and deciding whether or not one will try to fulfill one's moral ideal. Table 7 summarizes the environmental influences associated with this inner process. This process is influenced by overriding factors that affect one's self-esteem and willingness to risk oneself. They include mood states, motives, costs and benefits and one's own situational subjectivity.

Table 7

Situational Factors That Influence Component Three

Component 3

a) Select among competing value outcomes of ideals, the one to act on.

b) Deciding whether or not to try to fulfill one's moral ideal.
   Influences
   a) Factors that activate different motives, other than moral motives.
   b) Mood states that influence decision-making.
   c) Factors that influence estimates of costs and benefits.
   d) Factors that influence subjective estimates of the probability of certain occurrences.
   e) Factors that affect one's self-esteem and willingness to risk oneself, defensively reinterpreting the situation by blaming the victim, denying need or deservingness.

Note. Adapted from Rest, J.R. *The major components of morality* in Kurtines, W.M. & Gewirtz, J.L. (1984). *Morality, moral behavior, and moral development*. New York: John Wiley & Sons.

Situational Influences of Component 4

The fourth aspect of the inner processing of moral behavior consists of executing and implementing what one intends to do. Table 8 summarizes the environmental influences associated with this inner process. These processes include factors that physically prevent one from carrying out a moral plan of action, or factors that distract, fatigue, or disgust a person. Additionally, these influences include cognitive transformations of the goal and one's difficulties in managing more than one plan at a time.

Table 8

Situational Factors That Influence Component Four

Component 4

a) Execute and implement what one intends to do.

Influences

   a) Factors that physically prevent one from carrying out a moral plan of action.

   b) Factors that distract, fatigue, or disgust a person.

   c) Cognitive transformations of the goal.

   d) Timing difficulties in managing more than one plan at a time.

Note. Adapted from Rest, J.R. *The major components of morality* in Kurtines, W.M. & Gewirtz, J.L. (1984). *Morality, moral behavior, and moral development.* New York: John Wiley & Sons.

Having an overall understanding of the complexity that the components of the inner processes of moral behavior share with environmental perceptual cues and employee interactions, we become aware of situational individuality concerning one's moral structure and decision-making processes.

Moral Structure and Decision-Making

We have, in fact, two kinds of morality side by side: one which we preach but do not practice, and another which we practice but seldom preach.
— Bertrand Russell

I n a world that frequently places people in situations that require complex and difficult moral decisions, we often conclude that in the end, the responsibility for moral choices rests with the individual, not with systems or principles (Kurtines, 1984). Kurtines provides a conceptual framework in which rule-governed moral behavior is influenced by person and situational effects on moral choices and decisions.

Moral Structure

Kurtines (1984) states that previous literature on moral behavior that focuses on person variables is oversimplified and incomplete. He argues that there is a "...complex interaction that occurs between the person as moral agent, actor, and decision maker and the extensive network of socially defined rules and roles that make up social systems" (p. 304). He holds that "...morality is seen as performing a critical social function (systems maintenance and integration), and it is conceptualized as the network of rules that govern relations between individuals within a system" (p. 305).

In other words, Kurtines sees morality as an interaction between an individual and his or her social system based on the social system's defined roles and mores, not as one's personal belief system. In previous research, Frankena (cited in Kurtines, 1984) argued that "...there are at least two basic principles of morality, the principle of beneficence or utility and the principle of justice, that provide a rational organizational structure for rules and conventions normally associated with morality" (p. 307).

More specifically, one's principles are applied to the social system with relationship to perceived need. It is in this scope that Kurtines created a visual perspective of these relationships. By developing a systems-structural perspective, Kurtines (1984) adds, "...pragmatism (or instrumentalism) to this basic ethical position. The pragmatism principle defines an act or activity as good if it is more useful, practical, or efficient relative to alternative acts or activities" (p. 307-308).

According to Kurtines (1984), any individual act acquires meaning from the complex relationships between moral rules, rights and principles that makeup an underlying structure of morality (Figure 1).

> Utilizing to this approach, an individual's moral obligation is normally determined by the rules and conventions usually associated with morality, but in cases of conflict between the rules, the individual's moral obligation is determined by the rule that best fulfills the joint requirements of utility and justice. (p. 307)

By defining these relationships visually, it creates an understanding of one's "fit" within the structure of a social system. Kurtines' (1984) moral structure is termed "psychosocial role theory" in that it is based on three traditions in social theory. The three concepts that psychosocial role theory gets its heritage are, "...open systems theory... traditional role theory..." and "...a view of human behavior as rule-governed behavior" (p. 305).

Lastly, Kurtines' (1984) theoretical perspective assumes that human behavior is (1) rule governed, i.e., it conforms to rules (both explicit or implicit); (2) it is purposeful or intentional, i.e., it takes place within situations defined by goals, aims, outcomes and ends; (3) anthropomorphic, i.e., human beings are self-directed agents capable of employing a variety of rules; and (4) social, i.e., situation specific behavior takes place within a larger context.

Figure 1 depicts the structure of morality with two components: the surface structure and the underlying structure. The underlying structure embodies the principles ($PN_{1...n}$), rules ($R_{1...n}$) and rights and obligations ($RO_{1...n}$). It has three levels: rules and conventions, rights and obligations, and principles. The surface structure denotes one's ($P_{1...n}$) actions ($A_{1...n}$) over time ($T_{1...n}$). The underlying structure and surface structure are related as shown in Figure 1. One's actions over time are related to the various rules, rights and obligations based on the underlying principles that one holds consistent with their beliefs.

Figure 1 is a cornerstone in the understanding of how employees' underlying principles are related to their eventual actions. A comprehensive understanding of the underlying component relationships between principles, roles, rules and eventual actions is significant for us to understand the dynamic relationships employees face in today's ever-changing organizations.

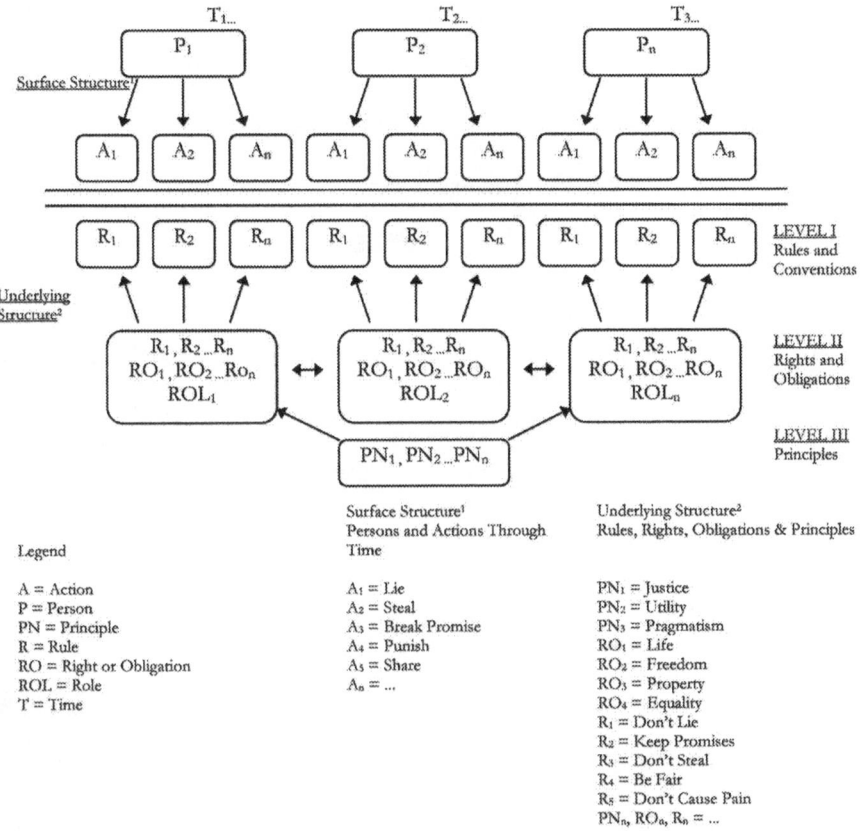

Figure 1. The Structure of Morality.

Note: Adapted from Kurtines, W.M. Moral behavior as rule-governed behavior: A psychosocial role-theoretical approach to moral behavior and development. In W.M. Kurtines & J.L. Gewirtz (Ed.) (1984). *Morality, moral behavior, and moral development*. New York: John Wiley & Sons.

Decision-Making

Kurtines (1984), after a thorough literature review (Kohlberg, 1969; Mischel & Mischel, 1976; Piaget, 1932/1965 cited in Kurtines, 1984), described decision-making from a systems perspective. He reported that "...situations involving a moral judgment require either a behavioral decision or a distributive decision" (p. 311). In other words, from a systems perspective, nothing is "an island unto itself"; theoretically, all components, or, subsystems are related somehow to all other subsystems within the system. As an example, employee A's behavior has an effect on employee B's perception of A.

Behavioral decisions involve decisions that regulate one's behavior. Some examples of these types of decisions are lying versus not lying and stealing versus not stealing. Additionally, Kurtines (1984) states that, "Behavioral decisions are teleological in that the consequence of the act tends to serve as the decision criterion" (p. 311)

Distributive decisions are decisions that require allocation of some sort of resources; and such a decision "...presents the decision maker with a choice between two or more possible distributions of some thing or activity within the system" (p. 311). In contrast to behavioral decisions, distributive decisions are seen as "...deontological in that the relative fairness (in the sense of equality or equity) of the distribution, rather than the consequences of the distribution, tends to serve as the decision criterion" (p. 311).

Kurtines' (1984) decision-making model includes research on situational effects, person effects, and person and situation effects on moral decision-making. The integration of the person and situation effects is argued from the view that, "Social systems are thus rooted in interactions between individuals, and a systems approach shifts the conceptual focus from the individual in isolation to the individual within a social context" (p. 316).

Kurtines' (1984) decision-making model (Figure 2) is referred to as the three-stage successive-hurdles model because it represents the "minimum number of sequential stages needed to arrive at a moral decision" (p. 310) as follows:

1. The selection and application of the appropriate Level I rules
2. A test for conflict between the rule and appropriate higher-order Level II moral right or obligation
3. A test for conflict between the right or obligation and the appropriate higher-order Level III moral principle

The three-stage model "...suggests that most moral decisions do not involve a moral 'dilemma'..." additionally, "...those decisions that do involve a 'dilemma' concern conflict between moral rules or conventions and 'higher-order' moral rights and obligations or moral principles" (p. 313). In other words, a moral dilemma is grounded in conflict between deontological versus teleological criterion.

Lastly, the model demonstrates that to judge a particular act or activity morally obligatory, "...the rule that prescribes or prohibits it must be consistent with at least one of the general principles of morality, but not necessarily all of them" (p.313).

Conflict between moral rules or conventions and "higher-order" moral rights and obligations or moral principles, as posited by Kurtines (1984), is also prevalent in recent research (Sims & Kroeck, 1994; Wimbush, Shepard & Markham, 1997; Sims & Keon, 2000). Wimbush, Shepard and Markham (1997) concluded that work climates are significant influences on employee behavior. Sims and Kroeck found that the "...ethical work climate is an important variable in the study of person-organization fit" (p. 946). Sims and Keon (2000) reported that perceived ethical choices are significantly related to role conflict experienced by employees.

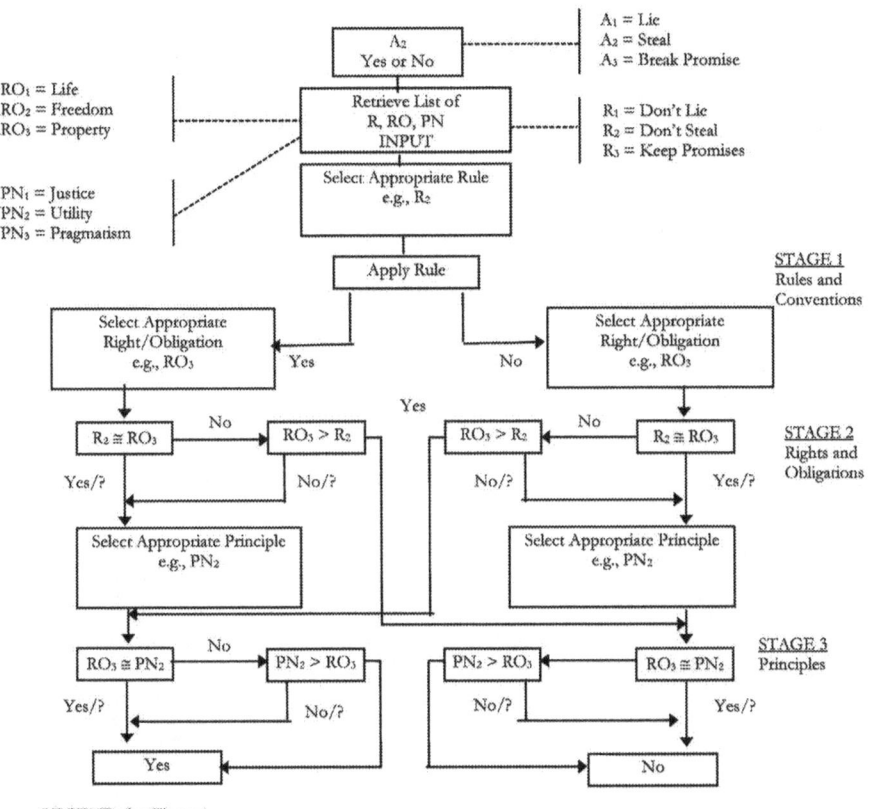

Figure 2. Three-Stage Successive Hurdles Moral Decision-Making Model.

Note: Adapted from Kurtines, W.M, Moral behavior as rule-governed behavior: A psychosocial role-theoretical approach to moral behavior and development. In W.M. Kurtines & J.L. Gewirtz (Ed.) (1984). *Morality, moral behavior, and moral development*. New York: John Wiley & Sons.

Chapter 4

The Ethical Environment, Ethical and Moral Climates

A man's ethical behavior should be based effectually on sympathy, education, and social ties; no religious basis is necessary. Man would indeed be in a poor way if he had to be restrained by fear of punishment and hope of reward after death.
– Albert Einstein

From a systemic perspective, climates can be viewed as subsystems of the overall system or ethical environment. Moral climates are defined as the overall normative systems or mores that guide organizational decision-making, whereas, ethical climates are made up of the employees' beliefs as exhibited through their various behaviors.

Treviño, Butterfield, and McCabe (1998) performed an exploratory factor analysis of various ethical contexts in organizations and found that ethical climate and ethical culture espouse different elements of ethical context. Ethical climate can be defined as "...those aspects of work climate that determine what constitutes ethical behavior at work" (p.448); whereas, ethical culture consists of formal and informal "...rules, codes, rewards, leadership, rituals, and stories" (p. 453). The study expands the nine ethical climate types posited by Cullen and Victor in an unpublished manuscript (1993).

Ethical Environment

Ethical environment encompasses ethical leadership, role modeling, ethical norms, reward systems that support ethical conduct, and identifies the degree to which unethical behavior is punished in organizations.

Ethical Climate

The nine ethical climate types identified by Cullen and Victor (cited in Treviño, Butterfield and McCabe, 1998, p. 448-449) include the:

1. Egoist-individual - self-interest is the expected norm
2. Egoistic-local - the company's interest guides the decisions that are made
3. Egoist-cosmopolitan – efficiency is the expected norm
4. Benevolent-individual – the welfare of individuals inside the organization guide decisions
5. Benevolent-local – the welfare of groups inside the organization guide decisions
6. Benevolent-cosmopolitan – the welfare of individuals and groups outside the organization guide decisions

7. Principled-individual – personal morals guide decisions
8. Principled-local – organizational rules and regulations are the norm
9. Principled-cosmopolitan – external laws and codes guide ethical decisions

The various ethical climates that were identified in the Treviño, Butterfield and McCabe (1998) study were employee-focused (benevolent-individual), community-focused (benevolent-cosmopolitan), obedience to authority (egoistic-local), code implementation (benevolent-local), self-interest (egoistic-individual), efficiency (egoist-cosmopolitan), rules and procedures (principled-local), personal ethics (principled-individual) and law and professional codes climate (principled-cosmopolitan).

In summary, Treviño, Butterfield and McCabe (1998) found that "...the ethical context of the organization is associated with employee attitudes and behavior" (p.470).

Moral Climate

Cohen (1998) states that, "...to identify the normative systems that guide organizational decision-making and the systemic responses to ethical dilemmas..." (p. 1212) however, while providing broad-based classification schemes, prior research "...did not specify what the practices and procedures might be" (p. 1212) that would truly operationalize the models.

Cohen (1998, p. 1213) identifies a moral climate typology that identifies the types of organizational decisions that include a moral component:

1. Deontological – organizational decisions with a moral component that concern intentions to fulfill constituent obligations or meet other social responsibilities.
2. Utilitarian/consequentialist – focus on the potentially harmful consequences that might result.
3. Contractarian – consider the existence of any implicit or explicit social contract to constitute a moral concern.
4. Distributive justice – emphasize the importance of fairly distributing benefits and burdens within the firm.
5. Procedural justice – concerned with the fairness of procedures for determining duties, rewards and punishments.

Thus, Cohen (1998) defines moral climate as prevailing employee perceptions of organizational signals about norms for establishing intentions, considering consequences, observing contracts, determining distribution and implementing procedures. Cohen (1998) also includes a multi-dimensionality component to her framework that includes five dimensions, goal emphasis, means emphasis, socio-emotional, task support and reward orientation. Lastly, one caveat that Cohen (1998) expresses is that "...climate for a certain behavior does not cause individuals to perform that behavior" (p. 1214).

Thus far, we have discussed the major issues associated with the construct of ethics and morality. This book seeks to extend relationships between ethical beliefs and behaviors as related to components of moral behavior and decision-making to provide an impetus for a model for ethical leadership. Pickett (2001) in a study between two organizations in similar industries; one that has won the Malcolm Baldrige National Quality Award (MB) and one that has not (Non-MB), found that;

> The MB group espoused a quality/standards-
> oriented, process-driven focus that, while not
> perfect, demonstrated efforts to adhere to nationally
> recognized quality standards. On the other hand, the
> Non-MB group did not display these efforts based on
> reported behaviors. Additionally, the Non-MB group,
> when contrasted with the MB group, lacked many of
> the beliefs that could lead to truly incorporating the
> ethical norms within an organization. More times
> than not, it displayed a façade or pretense of ethical
> norms that did not materialize from the reported
> observed behaviors. (p. 143)

In a subsequent empirical study, Pickett (2003) found that the decision-making processes were significantly affected by the aforementioned ethical and environmental variables. This book furthers Pickett's (2001; 2003) previous research by exploring how the relationships between employees' beliefs and observed behaviors relate to Rest's (1984) components of moral behavior and decision-making within organizations thereby providing the cornerstone of ethical leadership within today's organizations.

Chapter 5

Ethical Leadership: The Model

Leadership and learning are indispensable to each other.
— John F. Kennedy

thical Leadership sounds like a very illusive "pie-in-the-sky" sort of concept, however, given the evolution of our society, it is becoming an issue that needs to be attended to in today's organizations. I propose a 5-step model that, based on academic research, has the ability to truly provide organizations the wherewithal to apply the concepts that can revolutionize their methods of leadership and views of corporate social responsibility.

The Components of the Model

Taking a moment to view Figure 1, we see 5 distinct components that contribute to Ethical Leadership.

Figure 1. Model for Ethical Leadership ©2001 *Michael C. Pickett.*

Ethical Environment and Ethical Climates

Treviño, Butterfield and McCabe (1998) performed an exploratory factor analysis of various ethical contexts in organizations and found that ethical climate and ethical culture espouse different elements of ethical context. The study expands the nine ethical climate types posited by Cullen and Victor (1993; cited in Treviño, Butterfield and McCabe, 1998, p. 448-449) in an unpublished manuscript.

Ethical Environment. Ethical environment encompasses ethical leadership, role modeling, ethical norms, reward systems that support ethical conduct and identifies the degree to which unethical behavior is punished in organizations and contains various ethical climates.

Ethical Climate. The nine ethical climate types identified by Cullen and Victor (cited in Treviño, Butterfield and McCabe, 1998, p. 448-449) include the:

1. Egoist-individual - self-interest is the expected norm
2. Egoistic-local - the company's interest guides the decisions that are made
3. Egoist-cosmopolitan – efficiency is the expected norm
4. Benevolent-individual – the welfare of individuals inside the organization guide decisions
5. Benevolent-local – the welfare of groups inside the organization guide decisions
6. Benevolent-cosmopolitan – the welfare of individuals and groups outside the organization guide decisions
7. Principled-individual – personal morals guide decisions
8. Principled-local – organizational rules and regulations are the norm
9. Principled-cosmopolitan – external laws and codes guide ethical decisions

The various ethical climates that were identified in the Treviño, Butterfield and McCabe (1998) study were employee-focused (benevolent-individual), community-focused (benevolent-cosmopolitan), obedience to authority (egoistic-local), code implementation (benevolent-local), self-interest (egoistic-individual), efficiency (egoist-cosmopolitan), rules and procedures (principled-local), personal ethics (principled-individual) and law and professional codes climate (principled-cosmopolitan). In summary, Treviño,

Butterfield and McCabe (1998) found that "...the ethical context of the organization is associated with employee attitudes and behavior" (p.470).

Moral Climate. Cohen (1998), however, states that, "...to identify the normative systems that guide organizational decision-making and the systemic responses to ethical dilemmas..." (p. 1212), while providing broad-based classification schemes, prior research "...did not specify what the practices and procedures might be", (p. 1212) that would truly operationalize the models.

Cohen (1998, p. 1213) identifies a moral climate typology that identifies the types of organizational decisions that include a moral component:

1. Deontological – organizational decisions with a moral component that concern intentions to fulfill constituent obligations or meet other social responsibilities.
2. Utilitarian/consequentialist – focus on the potentially harmful consequences that might result.
3. Contractarian – consider the existence of any implicit or explicit social contract to constitute a moral concern.
4. Distributive justice – emphasize the importance of fairly distributing benefits and burdens within the firm.
5. Procedural justice – concerned with the fairness of procedures for determining duties, rewards and punishments.

Thus, Cohen (1998, p. 1213) defines moral climate as, prevailing employee perceptions of organizational signals about norms for establishing intentions, considering consequences, observing contracts, determining distribution and implementing procedures. Cohen (1998) also includes a multi-dimensionality component to her framework that includes five dimensions, goal emphasis, means emphasis, socio-emotional, task support and reward orientation. Lastly, one caveat that Cohen (1998) expresses is that "...climate for a certain behavior does not cause individuals to perform that behavior" (p. 1214).

Inner Processes of Moral Behavior. Rest (1984) argues that previous theoretical concerns in morality are grounded in three basic constructs of behavior, affect and cognition. Additionally, Rest (1984) posits that by segregating research into these three notions, research remains divided, and the "...three-part scheme is deficient for many reasons" (p. 25). In short, Rest (1984) proposed a four-component model identifying the inner processes producing behavior (Table 1).

Table 1
The Inner Processes of Moral Behavior

Component	Major Functions
1	a) Interpret the situation in terms of how one's actions affect the welfare of others.
2	a) Formulate what a moral course of action would be.
	b) Identify the moral ideal in a specific situation.
3	a) Select among competing value outcomes of ideals, the one to act on.
	b) Deciding whether or not to try to fulfill one's moral ideal.
4	a) Execute and implement what one intends to do.

Note: Adapted from Rest, J.R. *The major components of morality* in Kurtines, W.M. & Gewirtz, J.L. (1984). *Morality, moral behavior, and moral development.* New York: John Wiley & Sons.

Again, to review, while the four components of the inner processes of moral behavior appear to be linear in fashion, Rest (1984) disclaims that moral behavior is a "unitary process" and that moral behavior is a "...manifestation and result of four inner cognitive-affective processes" (p.29) and "...deficiencies in any component can result in failure to behave morally" (p. 36).

Corporate Social Responsibility. Carroll and Buchholtz (2000) argue a four-part definition of corporate social responsibility that includes the economic, legal, ethical and philanthropic perspectives of the organization. An organization's economic responsibilities include the notion to be profitable. Businesses are in the business of being profitable; to maximize sales revenues while attempting to minimize costs.

Legal responsibilities include the ideology that businesses obey all laws and regulations to include consumer and environmental laws. In addition, society expects businesses to fulfill all contractual obligations.

Society expects businesses to fulfill their ethical responsibilities by avoiding questionable practices that may not be codified into law and assume that the law is a "floor" of behavior and also adhere to the spirit of the law. Lastly, a business' philanthropic responsibilities are highly "desired" by society; however is not a perceived requirement by society of a business to pursue such activities.

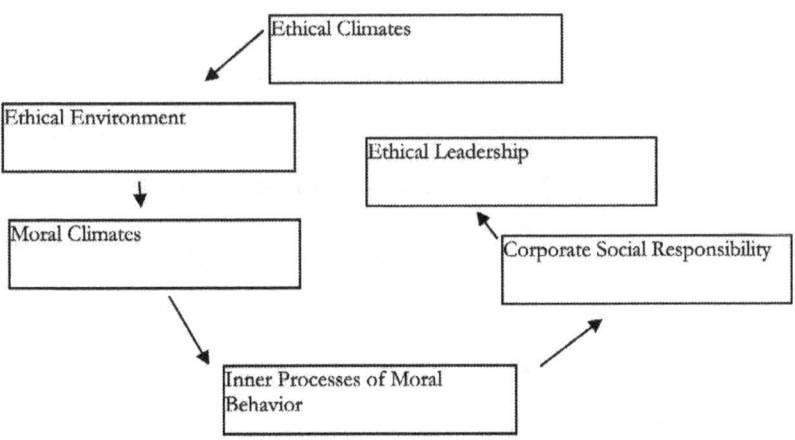

Figure 2. Process Model for Ethical Leadership. ©2001 *Michael C. Pickett.*

Process Model for Ethical Leadership

As depicted in Figure 2, ethical climates make up the overall ethical environment. The overall ethical environment gives rise to the various propensities for moral climates from which the every day operations of the organization takes place. The moral climates give rise to the conditions from which the decision-making processes in organizations are accomplished. These various decisions contain the components that make up the inner processes of moral behavior that lead to the organization's perceived corporate social responsibility. The extent of Ethical Leadership that an organization portrays is directed related to the make up of the previous components. As an example, for an organization to succeed at high levels of corporate social responsibility, they must first maintain an environment that allows for all four of the components of the inner processes of moral behavior to be present.

Thus, this model serves as somewhat of a prescriptive tool in that if an organization wishes to maintain Ethical Leadership, they must maintain high levels of corporate social responsibility; to do that, they must be able to accommodate the four of the components of the inner processes of moral behavior. As can be seen from the process model (Figure 2), ultimately, leaders and managers can evaluate the types of ethical climates that they need to espouse that will get them the overall behaviors that they truly want represented from within their organization.

Additionally, this model provides many provocative behavioral avenues from which to approach an organization. Reflecting on the old adage "Actions speak louder than words" rekindles the importance of how employees' behaviors take on a new meaning from within the context of an organization.

Ethical Leadership: The Model

As depicted in Figure 3, the Ethical Leadership Model consists of five quadrants labeled C1 through C5 in addition to the four inner processes of moral behavior (IPMB) labeled one through four. Each of the five quadrants consists of ethical climates, while only four of the five also contain relevant corporate social responsibility descriptors; the exception is quadrant C3, which provides a transition area between quadrants C4 and C2.

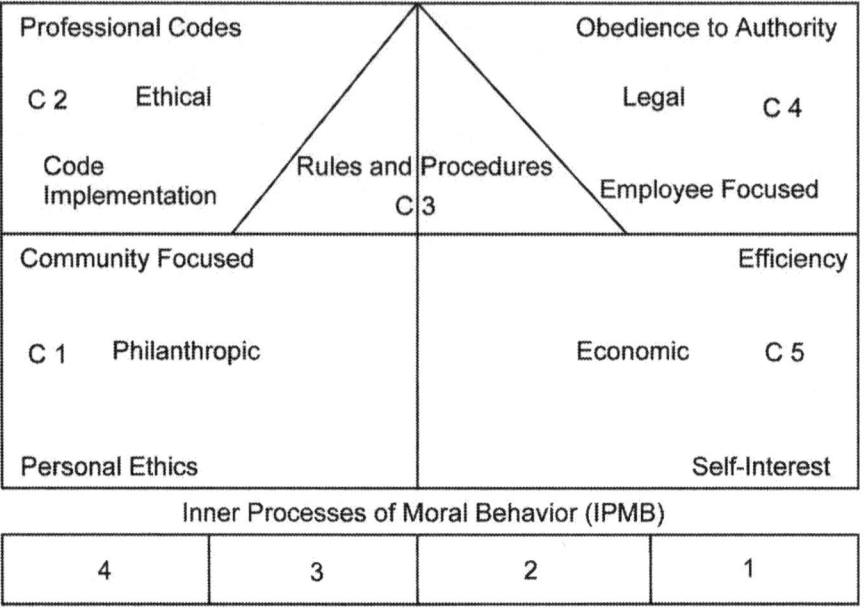

Figure 3. Ethical Leadership Model. ©2001 Michael C. Pickett.

Quadrant C5

This quadrant contains the ethical climates of self-interest and efficiency (Figure 3). Organizations that operate in these types of environments typically are not self-directed or self-actualized workgroups. Additionally, this area of the Ethical Leadership (EL) model only encompasses the inner-processes of moral behavior (IPMB) components 1 and 2; where employees may interpret the situation in terms of how one's actions affect the welfare of others and formulate what a moral course of action would be and maybe even identify the moral ideal in a specific situation, however, the guiding behaviors and decisions would be based on the overriding economic organizational concerns, individuated self-interest and efficient operations.

Quadrant C4

Quadrant C4 contains the employee-focused ethical climate (Figure 3). As organizations mature, they tend to move toward an employee-focus where obedience to authority and maintaining adherence to legal issues are prime concerns.

This quadrant relates to IPMB, components 1 and 2, similar to EL model quadrant C5.

Quadrant C3

This quadrant (Figure 3) provides a transition into the ethical arena for the organization. The obedience to authority and legal focuses turn into standardizations which eventually transitions into the categories of EL model quadrant C2 - professional codes, code implementations and an overall ethical focus for the organization. From an organizational structural perspective, this quadrant incorporates many of the beginning characteristics of Henry Mintzberg's professional bureaucracy (Mintzberg, 1979). Additionally, Bass (1990) further defines a bureaucracy as "...an organization that is operated on the basis of rules, regulations and orderliness and that focuses on legitimacy, the duties of jobs, and the rights of the office" (p. 916). Lastly, this area of the model incorporates IPMB 2 and 3 where leaders formulate what a moral course of action would be, identify the moral ideal in a specific situation, select among competing value outcomes of ideals, the one to act on, and deciding whether or not to try to fulfill one's moral ideal.

Quadrant C2

In quadrant C2 (Figure 3) ethical behavior is quantified by maintaining adherence to professional codes and the implementation of these codes. Many organizations operate within this quadrant. Society's view of these organizations is that the organization has participative management and maintains an atmosphere of professionalism.

Additionally, quadrant C2 may either incorporate IPMB components 3, 4 or both, in which employees select among competing value outcomes of ideals (the one to act on), decide whether or not to try to fulfill one's moral ideal and execute and implement what one intends to do.

Quadrant C1

Quadrant C1 (Figure 3) encompasses a community-focused climate where employees incorporate a high sense of personal ethics, in contrast to quadrant C2 where professional codes and their implementation define ethical behaviors. Personal ethics allows for individualism that rids the organizational mores of "leaving your ethics at the door when you come in". This quadrant also espouses philanthropic behavior in organizations when organizations participate in community-focused activities in order to promulgate goodwill.

At this level in the EL model, all four IPMB components are present truly permitting for leaders to select among competing value outcomes of ideals (the one to act on), decide whether or not to try to fulfill one's moral ideal and execute and implement what one intends to do.

Chapter 6

Achieving Strategic Corporate Sustainability: The Integration of Ethical Leadership

Do not go where the path may lead, go instead where there is no path and leave a trail.
– Ralph Waldo Emerson

The concept of strategic management can be traced back to H. Igor Ansof, considered the father of strategic management. Ansof suggests that during times of turbulent environments, organizations are able to develop strategic contingencies can be anticipated and planned for by organizations. In contrast, Henry Mintzberg suggests that organizations cannot utilize strategic management in turbulent environmental conditions (personal communication, 1998, Academy of Management). In either case, whether or not it is discernable to strategically operate one's organization in turbulent environmental conditions, the concept of corporate social responsibility is an important recent component of the strategic management field that is receiving much attention (Wheelen & Hunger, 2000).

Corporate Social Responsibility and Strategic Management

Carroll (1999) traced the concept of corporate social responsibility (CSR) back to a publication by Bowen that addressed the specific concept of social responsibility and is considered the father of CSR (Carroll, 1999). As CSR progressed, it became a realization that organizations must have a societal component to their overall strategic developmental processes. According to Steiner (1971), business is and must remain fundamentally as economic institution, but it does have responsibilities to help society achieve its basic goals and does, therefore, have social responsibilities. The larger a company becomes, the greater are these responsibilities, but all companies can assume some share of them at no cost and often at a short-run as well as a long-run profit.

The assumption of social responsibilities is more of an attitude, of the way a manager approaches his decision-making task, than a great shift in the economics decision making. It is a philosophy that looks at eh social interest and the enlightened self-interest of business over the long run as compared to the old, narrow, unrestrained short-run self-interest (P. 164). As argued by Steiner, it is very evident that the concept of CSR is well-defined construct that is becoming an essential cornerstone in corporate strategic theory.

Many organizations are finding the strategic social context of organizations to be critical links between external relations and profitability (Epstein & Westbrook, 2001), benchmarking technology issues (Roberts, 2001), using virtue theory as a strategic dynamic is ethical business development (Arjoon, 2000) and as a developmental extension as a model for venture growth (Baum et al, 2001).

Additionally, Rowe (2001) delineates critical role differentiations between strategic leaders, visionary leaders and managerial leaders. Some of the characteristics that Rowe (2001) identifies include, a synergistic combination of managerial and visionary leadership, an emphasis on ethical behavior and value-based decisions, an ability to formulate and implement strategies for immediate impact and preservation of long-term goals to enhance organizational survival, growth and long-term viability.

Lastly, Husted (2000) developed a contingency theory of corporate social performance that includes a functional fit between social issues, the organizational structure and corresponding strategies. This "fit" will allow organizational strategists to properly develop the "...appropriate organizational responses to different kinds of social issues and in the diagnoses of resolution of mismatches..." (p. 43) between the organizational structure, strategy and social issue.

Integration: Ethical Leadership and Strategy Formulation

According to Thompson and Strickland (2001), the factors, both internal and external, contribute to shaping the choice of a company's strategy (Figure 4).

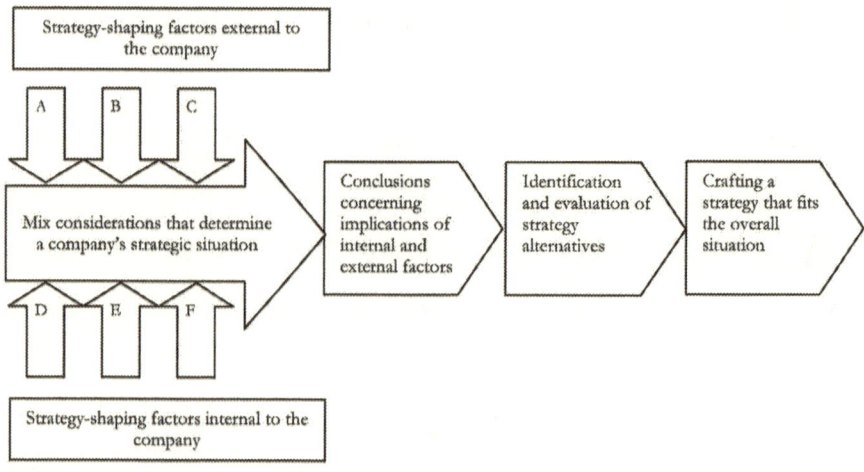

Figure 4. Factors Shaping the Choice of Company Strategy. Source: Adapted from Thompson & Strickland (2001).

Strategy-Shaping Factors External to the Company

The first group of external factors that contribute to shaping a company's strategy are economic, societal, regulatory, and community considerations (A) that are related to quadrants C4 (legal) and C5 (economic) of the EL model (Figure 3). These two quadrants encompass a portion of the intent of Carroll and Buckholz's (2000) CSR model, a four-part definition of corporate social responsibility that includes the economic, legal, ethical and philanthropic perspectives of the organization. The integration of this notion is clearly a meaningful beginning from which to approach strategy development.

The second group of external factors (B) includes competitive conditions and overall industry attractiveness that is approached from clearly an organizational self-interest perspective corresponding to Quadrant C5, containing the ethical climates of self-interest and efficiency (Figure 3). This portion of the EL model only encompasses the inner-processes of moral behavior (IPMB) components 1 and 2; where employees may interpret the situation in terms of how one's actions affect the welfare of others based on the overriding economic organizational concerns, individuated self-interest and efficient operations.

The last group of external factors (C) includes the company's opportunities & threats to the company's well being. According to Thompson and Strickland (2001), "A company's strategy needs to be deliberately aimed at capturing its best growth opportunities, especially the ones that hold the most promise for building sustainable growth opportunities" (p. 62). As such, Quadrant C3, Rules and Procedures, operationally describe Thompson and Strickland's strategic intent. As a hierarchical organization, it operates based on regulation and orderliness as cited previously by Bass (1990).

Strategy-Shaping Factors Internal to the Company

The first internal factor (D) mentioned by Thompson and Strickland (2001) is a company's resource strengths, weaknesses, competencies and competitive capabilities (Figure 4). This internal factor is also comprised in Quadrant C3 Rules and Procedures. Additionally, as Thompson and Strickland (2001) share Quadrant C3 with both an internal and external factor, it is this "internal" component that takes advantage of the EL model's IPMB 2 and 3 (Figure 3), where leaders formulate what a moral course of action would be, identify the moral ideal in a specific situation, select among competing value outcomes of ideals, the one to act on, and deciding whether or not to try to fulfill one's moral ideal.

Thompson and Strickland's (2001) second internal factor (E) that contributes to shaping and organization's strategy include personal ambitions, business philosophies, and ethical principles of key executives (Figure 4). This factor clearly incorporates the notion of Quadrant C2 (Figure 3) including Carroll and Buchholtz's (2000) CSR component and the ethical climates of professional codes and code implementation. Also this factor operationalizes the EL model's IMPB 3 and the first component of IMPB 4 (Figure 3), electing among competing value outcomes of ideals the one to act on, deciding whether or not to try to fulfill one's moral ideal.

The last internal factor (F) mentioned by Thompson and Strickland (2001) include the notions of shared values and company culture (Figure 4). According to Thompson and Strickland (2001):

> Typically, the stronger a company's culture, the more
> that culture is likely to shape a company's strategic
> actions, sometimes even dominating the choice
> of strategic moves. This is because culture-related
> values and beliefs are so embedded in management's
> strategic thinking and actions that they condition
> how the enterprise does business and responds to
> external events. (p. 63)

It is with this socially relevant concept of acting on one's strategy that encompasses the final Quadrant C1 of the EL model (Figure 3) that includes the ethical notions of community focus and employees' personal ethics. While Quadrant C1 includes IMPB 3 and 4, this is the time the second component of IMPB 4 is operationalized when the company executes and implements what one intends to do. Until this point, according the Thompson and Strickland (2001) model, the company had not acted on any strategic choices.

Once all factors have been considered, Thompson and Strickland (2001) come to their conclusion and define their implications, evaluate their alternatives, and develop the strategy the fits the overall situation (Figure 4).

As presented the compatibility of the two models render an organization a definite and unambiguous direction from which to begin in the ever-illusive challenge of strategy formulation. An organization's ability to achieve its long-term goals is espoused to internal behavioral processes and managerial abilities, has presented an integration of Ethical Leadership and strategic management. In other words, the integration of Ethical Leadership and strategic management planning creates a synergistic combination of managerial and visionary leadership, which serves to enhance organizational survival, growth, and long-term viability.

Chapter

7

The Future of Ethical Leadership

The beginning is the most important part of the work.
– Plato

The future of Ethical Leadership? This question reminds me of an interesting and appropriate anecdote concerning an organization's perceived needs versus reality. Upon reflection, early in my research, I had offered an organization the opportunity to take a closer look at their ethical climates utilizing my research instruments thereby affording them the ability to view the organization through the eyes of the Ethical Leadership model. As fate would have it, after several conversations with directors in departments such as Human Resources, Leadership Training & Development and the Ethics Department; all concluded that administering "another" survey was not needed. In fact, they all felt that they did not need any more "ethics or leadership training"; as the employees were already receiving ongoing leadership and ethics training and "more surveys are not needed."

Well . . . to make a very long story short, recently the president and vice-president had been dismissed on an ethics-related incident in addition to the CEO having to resign as well. Plato's words seem to ring as true today as they ever have undoubtedly *the beginning is the most important part of the work!*

Where to Start?

All organizations differ in their structures and management practices, however, as the saying goes – when you do not know where you are going, any road will get you there. The Ethical Leadership model offers a sound and competitive approach for those wishing to have a holistic and socially responsible grounded leadership philosophy. Understanding where you are within the Ethical Leadership model offers a wealth of information for you to discover and subsequently determine what is needed in your organization to produce your own road map toward achieving your goals as a dynamic and holistic learning organization that espouses the foundation of ethical leadership.

Designing Your Roadmap

Like any sustainable organizational change, you need to know where you are as it relates to where you want to be. A grounded understanding in visualizing your organization's end state is the one factor that separates successful change from those organizations that repeatedly fail in their attempts to maintain a successful momentum in their change processes (See Figure 5).

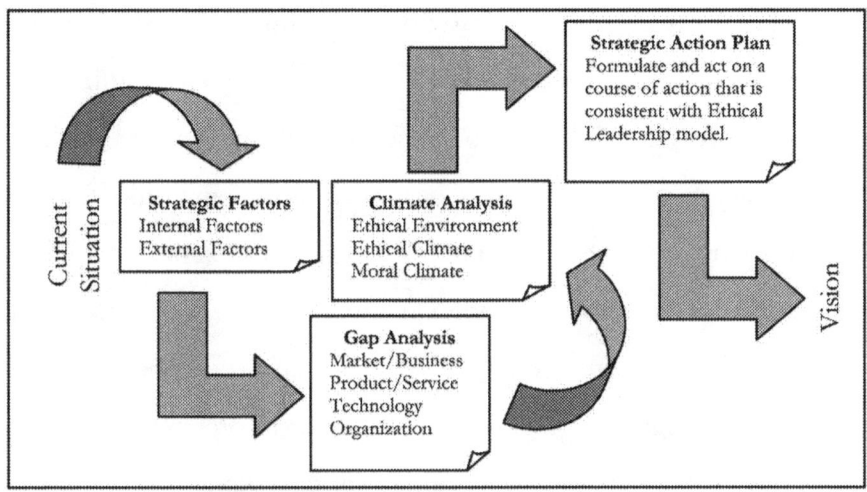

Figure 5. Ethical Leadership Strategic Roadmap. ©2005 *Michael C. Pickett*

Beginning with the understanding of your current situation with respect to your internal and external strategic factors your organization then prepares the in-depth gap analysis in defining, or re-defining your critical success factors and/or core values pertaining to your vision. With your new understanding of your strategic focus though the gap analysis, you then precede to determine the climate analysis within your organization. An abbreviated version is provided within this book as an example to determine your ethical climate (Appendix A). A complete statistical climate analysis which includes the environmental, ethical and moral instruments is available through the author's organization (Appendix B). If, upon completion of your ethical climate analysis, you see a need to for your organization to transition into another quadrant to achieve your strategic goals, methods are available to aid in the cultural transition process. Once your organization develops an understanding of the ethical environment, ethical and moral climates, you are then able to formulate a course of action that is consistent with your organization's ethical culture that will enable you to successfully implement Quadrant C1 (Chapter 5, Figure 3) which encompasses a community-focused climate where employees incorporate a high sense of personal ethics and personal ethics allows for individualism that rids the organizational mores of "leaving your ethics at the door when you come in". This quadrant also espouses philanthropic behavior in organizations when organizations participate in community-focused activities in order to promulgate goodwill. In addition all four IPMB components are present; truly permitting for leaders to select among competing value outcomes of ideals (the one to act on), decide whether or not to try to fulfill one's moral ideal and execute and implement what one intends to do.

APPENDIX A

Ethical Climate Assessment	Disagree	Somewhat Disagree	Somewhat Agree	Agree
Group 1	-3	-2	1	2
The effect of decisions on the customer and the public are a primary concern in this organization.				
People in this organization are actively concerned about the customer's and the public's interest.				
It is expected that you will do what is right for the customer and public.				
People in this organization have a strong sense of responsibility to the outside community.				
In this organization, people are guided by their own personal ethics.				
Each person in this organization decides for themselves what is right and wrong.				
The most important concern in this organization is each person's own sense of right and wrong.				
Total ⇨				
Group 2				
Employees are required to acknowledge that they have read and understood the ethics code.				
The organization has established procedures for employees to ask questions about ethics code requirements.				
The code of conduct is widely distributed throughout the organization.				
Employees are regularly required to assert that their actions are in compliance with the ethics code.				
In this organization, people are expected to comply with the law and professional standards over and above other considerations.				
In this organization, people are expected to strictly follow legal or professional standards.				
Total ⇨				
Group 3				
It is important to follow strictly the organization's rules and procedures.				
Everyone is expected to stick by company rules and procedures.				
Total ⇨				

(Table Continues)

Group 4				
The most important concern is the people in this organization.				
People are very concerned about what is generally best for employees in this organization.				
Our major consideration is what is best for everyone in this organization.				
What is best for each individual is a primary concern in this organization.				
It is expected that each individual is cared for when making decisions here.				
In this organization, people look out for each others' good				
This organization demands obedience to authority figures, without question.				
People in this organization are expected to do as they are told.				
The boss is always right in this organization.				
Total ⇨				

Group 5				
People in this organization are very concerned about what is best for themselves.				
In this organization, people protect their own interests above other considerations.				
In this organization, each person is expected above all to work efficiently.				
The major responsibility of people in this organization is to consider efficiency first.				
Efficient solutions to problems are always sought here.				
The most efficient way is always the right way in this organization.				
Total ⇨				

Group Totals

	A	B	C	D
Group 1 (C1) Totals ⇨				
			Total ⇨ C1	
Group 2 (C2) Totals ⇨				
			Total ⇨ C2	
Group 3 (C3) Totals ⇨				
			Total ⇨ C3	
Group 4 (C4) Totals ⇨				
			Total ⇨ C4	
Group 5 (C5) Totals ⇨				
			Total ⇨ C5	

Transpose the scores from the Ethical Climate Assessment to the respective Group totals.

Then add the group totals to get a group score.

©2005 Michael C. Pickett

Ethical Climates - Charting Your Scores

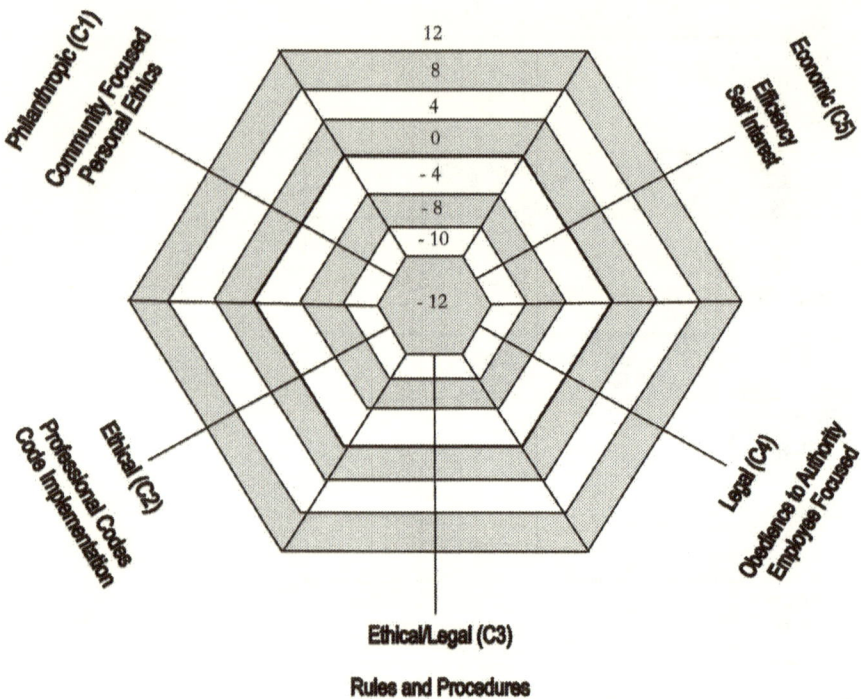

©2005 Michael C. Pickett

EXAMPLE Ethical Climate Assessment	Disagree	Somewhat Disagree	Somewhat Agree	Agree
Group 1	-3	-2	1	2
The effect of decisions on the customer and the public are a primary concern in this organization.		✓		
People in this organization are actively concerned about the customer's and the public's interest.		✓		
It is expected that you will do what is right for the customer and public.				
People in this organization have a strong sense of responsibility to the outside community.	✓			
In this organization, people are guided by their own personal ethics.	✓			
Each person in this organization decides for themselves what is right and wrong.		✓		
The most important concern in this organization is each person's own sense of right and wrong.		✓		
Total ⇨	-6	-8		
Group 2				
Employees are required to acknowledge that they have read and understood the ethics code.			✓	
The organization has established procedures for employees to ask questions about ethics code requirements.		✓		
The code of conduct is widely distributed throughout the organization.			✓	
Employees are regularly required to assert that their actions are in compliance with the ethics code.		✓		
In this organization, people are expected to comply with the law and professional standards over and above other considerations.				✓
In this organization, people are expected to strictly follow legal or professional standards.				✓
Total ⇨		-4	2	4

(Table Continues)

Group 3				
It is important to follow strictly the organization's rules and procedures.				✓
Everyone is expected to stick by company rules and procedures.				✓
Total ⇨				4
Group 4				
The most important concern is the people in this organization.		✓		
People are very concerned about what is generally best for employees in this organization.		✓		
Our major consideration is what is best for everyone in this organization.		✓		
What is best for each individual is a primary concern in this organization.	✓			
It is expected that each individual is cared for when making decisions here.			✓	
In this organization, people look out for each others' good		✓		
This organization demands obedience to authority figures, without question.				✓
People in this organization are expected to do as they are told.				✓
The boss is always right in this organization.				✓
Total ⇨	-3	-8	1	6
Group 5				
People in this organization are very concerned about what is best for themselves.				✓
In this organization, people protect their own interests above other considerations.				✓
In this organization, each person is expected above all to work efficiently.				✓
The major responsibility of people in this organization is to consider efficiency first.				✓
Efficient solutions to problems are always sought here.			✓	
The most efficient way is always the right way in this organization.				✓
Total ⇨			1	10

EXAMPLE

Group Totals

	A	B	C	D
Group 1 (C1) Totals ⇨	-6	-8		
			Total ⇨ C1	-14
Group 2 (C2) Totals ⇨		-4	2	4
			Total ⇨ C2	2
Group 3 (C3) Totals ⇨			4	
			Total ⇨ C3	4
Group 4 (C4) Totals ⇨	-3	-8	1	6
			Total ⇨ C4	-4
Group 5 (C5) Totals ⇨		1	10	
			Total ⇨ C5	11

EXAMPLE
Ethical Climates - Charting Your Scores

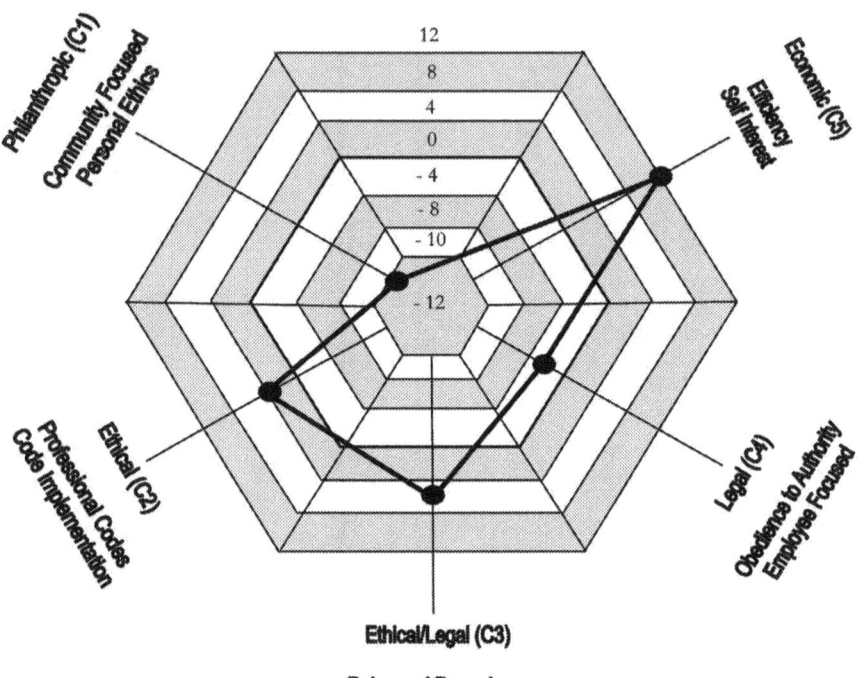

©2005 Michael C. Pickett

EXAMPLE
Ethical Climate Analysis

C5 – This organization seems to be highly skewed in the ethical climates of self-interest and efficiency (Figure 3). Organizations that operate in these types of environments typically are not self-directed or self-actualized workgroups. Additionally, this area of the Ethical Leadership (EL) model only encompasses the inner-processes of moral behavior (IPMB) components 1 and 2; where employees may interpret the situation in terms of how one's actions affect the welfare of others and formulate what a moral course of action would be and maybe even identify the moral ideal in a specific situation, however, the guiding behaviors and decisions would be based on the overriding economic organizational concerns, individuated self-interest and efficient operations.

C4 – In Quadrant C4 (Figure 3), this organization, scoring a -4, is moderately deficient in the areas of being employee-focused. Typically, as organizations mature, they tend to move toward an employee-focus where obedience to authority and maintaining adherence to legal issues are prime concerns. However, again referring to their highly skewed C5 scores, the organization is most likely strong in the obedience to authority and lacking in the employee-focused arena as it relates to individuated levels of self-interest. Again, this quadrant relates to IPMB, components 1 and 2, similar to EL model quadrant C5; where employees may interpret the situation in terms of how one's actions affect the welfare of others and formulate what a moral course of action would be and maybe even identify the moral ideal in a specific situation, however, the guiding behaviors and decisions would be based on the overriding economic organizational concerns, individuated self-interest and efficient operations.

C3 – In Quadrant C3 (Figure 3) this organization slightly increases involvement in the combination of the ethical (C2) and legal (C4) moving from the legal to the ethical quadrants indicating an involvement in the establishment of rules and procedures, but not to a great extent. In essence, this organization is growing in this transition from obedience to authority and legal focuses into standardizations. Lastly, this area of the model incorporates IPMB 2 and 3 where leaders formulate what a moral course of action would be, identify the moral ideal in a specific situation, select among competing value outcomes of ideals, the one to act on, and deciding whether or not to try to fulfill one's moral ideal.

C2 – In Quadrant C2 (Figure 3) this organization relaxes somewhat in the implementation of the standardizations implemented in the previous quadrant. In this quadrant, ethical behavior is quantified by maintaining adherence to professional codes and the implementation of these codes this indicated that this organization has participative management and maintains an atmosphere of professionalism. Additionally, this organization marginally incorporates IPMB components 3 and 4 indicating that employees may select among competing value outcomes of ideals, but may or may not execute and implement what one intends to do.

C1 – In Quadrant C1 (Figure 3), this organization is extremely weak, indicating a complete deficit of a community-focused climate where employees incorporate a high sense of personal ethics. Additionally, this organization lacks the qualities of firms that allows for individualism that rids the organizational mores of "leaving your ethics at the door when you come in". With this organizations high emphasis on efficiency, self-interest and economics (C5), it is fairly easy to see that there is no time for truly accomplishing strategies that allows for philanthropic behavior and participation in community-focused activities in order to promulgate goodwill.

APPENDIX B

For further questions or inquiries feel free to contact Dr. Pickett.

Pickett Training & Development

mpickett@ptd-inc.com

References

Anonymous. (1997). Unethical acts rampant, U.S. study finds. *Worklife Report, 10* (3), 18.

Bass, B.M. (1990). *Bass & Stogdill's handbook of leadership: theory, research, and managerial applications.* (3rd ed.). New York: The Free Press.

Bolman, L.G., Deal, T.D. (1997). *Reframing organizations: artistry, choice, and leadership.* San Francisco: Jossey-Bass.

Boyce, W.D. & Jenson, L.C. (1978). *Moral reasoning: a psychological-philosophical integration.* Lincoln, NB: University of Nebraska Press.

Baldrige National Quality Program. (2000). Criteria for performance excellence. (n.d.). Retrieved December 10, 2000, from http://www.quality.nist.gov/bcpg.pdf.htm#BUSINESS

Bridges, W. (1991). *Managing transitions: making the most out of change.* Reading, MA: Addison-Wesley.

Butcher, W.C. (1997). Ethical leadership. *Executive Excellence 14,* (6), 5-6.

Carlson, D.S. & Perrewe, P.L. (1995). Institutionalization of organizational ethics through transformational leadership. *Journal of Business Ethics 14,* (10), 829-838.

Carroll, A.B. (1996). *Business & society: ethics and stakeholder management.* (3rd ed.). Cincinnati: Southwestern College Publishing.

Chandler, J. (1996). *A workbook for ethics: course # ed 724.20.* Oklahoma City: CAPCO.

Ciulla, J.B. Leadership and the problem of bogus empowerment. (n.d.). Retrieved June 12, 2000, from http:// civicsource.org/klsp/klspdocs/jciul_p1.htm

Cohen, D.V. (1998). Moral climate in business firms: A conceptual framework for analysis and change. *Journal of Business Ethics 16,* (17), 1211-1226.

Covey, S.R. (1991). *Principle-centered leadership.* New York: Simon & Schuster, Inc.

Covey, S.R. (1997). Ethical vertigo. *Executive Excellence, 14* (6), 3-4.

Dingley, J.C. (1997). Durkheim, Mayo, morality and management. *Journal of Business Ethics 16,* (11), 1117-1129.

Donham, W.B. (1992). Business ethics - a general survey. *Harvard Business Review 70,* (5), 160.

Driscol, D. & Hoffman, M.W. Allow employees to speak out on company practices. *Workforce, 76* (11), 73-76.

Duska, R. & Whelan, M. (1975). Moral development: *A guide to Piaget and Kohlberg.* New York: Paulist Press.

Fort, T.L. (1997). How relationality shapes business and its ethics. *Journal of Business Ethics 16,* (12/13), 1381-1391.

Frankena, W.K. (1973). *Ethics.* Englewood Cliffs, NJ: Prentice-Hall.

Gini, A. (1997). Moral leadership: An overview. *Journal of Business Ethics 16,* (3), 323-330.

Gini, A. Moral leadership and business ethics. (n.d.). Retrieved January, 10 2001, from http://civicsource.org/klsp/klspdocs/agini_p1.htm.

Greengard, S. 50% of your employees are lying, cheating & stealing. *Workforce, 76* (10), 44-50.

Hair, F., Anderson, R., Tatham, R. & Black, W. (1998). *Multivariate data analysis.* (5th ed.). Upper Saddle River, NJ: Prentice-Hall.

Hersey, P., Blanchard, K.H. (1988). *Management of organizational behavior: utilizing human resources.* (5th ed.). Englewood Cliffs, NJ: Prentice-Hall.

Joseph, J.D. & Satish, P. (1997). The impact of ethical climate on job satisfaction of nurses. *Health Care Management Review, 22* (1), 76-81.

Koestenbaum, P. (1991). *Leadership: the inner side of greatness: a philosophy for leaders.* San Francisco: Jossey-Bass, Inc.

Kohlberg, L., Levine, C. & Hewer, A. (1983). *Moral stages: a current formulation and a response to critics.* Basil, Switzerland: S. Karger.

Kurtines, W.M, Moral behavior as rule-governed behavior: A psychosocial role-theoretical approach to moral behavior and development. In W.M. Kurtines & J.L. Gewirtz (Ed.) (1984). *Morality, moral behavior, and moral development.* New York: John Wiley & Sons.

Mason, E.S. & Mudrack, P.E. (1997). Do complex moral reasoners experience greater ethical work conflict? *Journal of Business Ethics, 16* (12/13), 1311-1318.

Maynard, R. Leading by example may promote worker honesty. *Nation's Business, 85* (9), 16.

McKeon, R. (1970). (ed.) *The basic works of Aristotle.* New York: Random House.

McShulskis, E. (1997). Job stress can prompt unethical behavior. *HRMagazine, 42* (7), 22-24.

Metzger, M.B. & Dalton, D.R. (1996). Seeing the elephant: an organizational perspective on corporate moral agency. *American Business Law Journal, 33* (4), 489-576.

Modgil, S. & Modgil, C. (eds.). (1986). *Lawrence Kolberg: consensus and controversy.* Philadelphia: The Falmer Press.

Navran, F. (1997a). Are your employees cheating to keep up? *Workforce, 76* (8), 58-62.

Navran, F. (1997b). 12 steps to building a best-practices ethics program. *Workforce, 76* (9), 117-121.

Patton, M.Q. (1996). *Utilization-focused evaluation: the new century text.* (3rd ed.). Thousand Oaks, CA: Sage.

Paul, J. & Strbiak, C.A. (1997). The ethics of strategic ambiguity. *Journal of Business Communication, 34* (2), 149-159.

Pickett, M.C. (2001). An exploratory analysis of the relationships between ethical beliefs and behavior within organizations. Unpublished Ed.D. doctoral dissertation. Pepperdine University, Malibu CA.

Pickett, M.C. (2003). Analysis and structure of ethical organizational relationships: The construct of ethical climates, environments, moral reasoning, and observed behaviors. Unpublished manuscript.

Popisil, V. (1997). Ethics check. *Industry Week*, 246 (17), 36.

Rest, J.R. (1979). *Development in judging moral issues.* Minneapolis, MN: University of Minnesota.

Rest, J.R. (1984). The major components of morality. In Kurtines, W.M. & Gewirtz, J.L. (1984). *Morality, moral behavior, and moral development.* New York: John Wiley & Sons.

Robbins, S.P. (1990). *Organization theory: structure, design and applications.* (3rd ed.). Englewood Cliffs, NJ: Prentice-Hall.

Rokeach, M. (1973). *The nature of human values.* New York: The Free Press.

Schwepker, C.H. Jr., Ferrell, O.C. & Ingram, T.N. (1997). The influence of ethical climate and ethical conflict on role stress in the sales force. *Journal of Academy of Marketing Science 25,* (2), 99-108.

Scminke, M. & Ambrose, M.L. (1997). Asymmetric perceptions of ethical frameworks of men and women in business and nonbusiness settings. *Journal of Business Ethics, 16* (7), 719-729.

Senge, P.M. (1990). *The fifth discipline: the art and practice of a learning organization.* New York: Doubleday.

Senge, P.M., Keiner, A., Roberts, C., Ross, R.B., & Smith, B.J. (1994). *The fifth discipline fieldbook: strategies and tools for building a learning organization.* New York: Doubleday.

Sims, R.L. & Kroeck, K.G. (1994). The influence of ethical fit on employee satisfaction, commitment and turnover. *Journal of Business Ethics 13,* 939-947.

Sims, R.L. & Keon, T.L. (1997). Ethical work climate as a factor in the development of person-organization fit. *Journal of Business Ethics 16,* 1095-1105.

Sims, R.L. & Keenan, J.P. (1998). Predictors of external whistleblowing: Organizational intrapersonal variables. *Journal of Business Ethics 17,* 411-421.

Sims, R.L. & Keon, T.L. (1999). Determinants of ethical decision making: The relationship of the perceived organizational environment. *Journal of Business Ethics 19,* 393-410.

Sims, R.L. & Keon, T.L. (2000). The influence of organizational expectations on ethical decision making conduct. *Journal of Business Ethics 23,* 219-228.

Snell, R.S., Taylor, K.F. & Chak, A. (1997). Ethical dilemmas and ethical reasoning: a study in Hong Kong. *Human Resource Management Journal, 7* (3), 19-30.

Street, M.D.R., Geiger, C. (1997). Ethical decision making: the effects of escalating commitment. *Journal of Business Ethics, 16* (11), 1153-1161.

Soloman, C.M. (1996). Prepare to walk a moral tightrope: put your ethics to a global test. *Personnel Journal, 75* (1), 66-72.

Soloman, R.C. Ethical leadership, emotions, and trust beyond "charisma". (n.d.). Retrieved on July 15, 2000, from http://civicsource.org/klsp/klspdocs/rsolo_p1.htm

Treviño, L.K., Butterfield, K.D. & McCabe, D.L. (1998). The ethical context in organizations: Influences on employee attitudes and behaviors. *Business Ethics Quarterly 8*, (3), 447-476.

Victor, B. & Cullen J.B. (1988). The organizational bases of ethical work climates. *Administrative Science Quarterly 33*, 101-125.

Weber, J. (1995). Influences upon organizational subclimates: A multi-departmental analysis of a single firm. *Organization Science 6*, (5), 509-523.

Wheatley, M.J. (1994). *Leadership and the new science.* San Francisco, CA: Berrett-Koehler.

Wyld, D.C. & Jones, C.A. (1997). The importance of context: The ethical work climate construct and models of ethical decision making -- an agenda for research. *Journal of Business Ethics 16*, (4), 465-472.

Yukl, G.A. (1989). *Leadership in organizations.* Englewood Cliffs, NJ: Prentice-Hall.

About the Author

Dr. Pickett has completed extensive research in organizational ethics and has published numerous articles relating to organizational strategy, ethics, and leadership. Dr. Pickett's educational background includes business, human resource management, organizational psychology, human behavior, leadership and technology. This diverse educational background has provided Dr. Pickett with a well-rounded foundation and holistic understanding of today's organizations.

Dr. Pickett served in the United States Marine Corps and has held several management positions in industry and is currently an organizational consultant and educator residing in Riverside, California with his wife Evette and daughter Jenna.

www.ingramcontent.com/pod-product-compliance
Lightning Source LLC
Chambersburg PA
CBHW022103170526
45157CB00004B/1460